RISE BEYOND ORDINARY, HEAL BEYOND BODY!

Tips & Remedies

ACHARYA PRERNA A JAIN

BlueRose ONE
Stories Matter
NewDelhi • London

BLUEROSE PUBLISHERS
India | U.K.

Copyright © Acharya Prerna A Jain 2024

All rights reserved by author. No part of this publication may be reproduced, stored in a retrieval system or transmitted in any form or by any means, electronic, mechanical, photocopying, recording or otherwise, without the prior permission of the author. Although every precaution has been taken to verify the accuracy of the information contained herein, the publisher assume no responsibility for any errors or omissions. No liability is assumed for damages that may result from the use of information contained within.

BlueRose Publishers takes no responsibility for any damages, losses, or liabilities that may arise from the use or misuse of the information, products, or services provided in this publication.

For permissions requests or inquiries regarding this publication, please contact:

BLUEROSE PUBLISHERS
www.BlueRoseONE.com
info@bluerosepublishers.com
+91 8882 898 898
+4407342408967

ISBN: 978-93-5819-738-9

Cover design: Tahira
Typesetting: Tanya Raj Upadhyay

First Edition: February 2024

Hi,

Atma Namaste!

This is PRERNA A JAIN.

An ordinary girl from a middle-class family who got married at the age of 18 without even completing primary education and after my marriage, My life changed with full of responsibility and family to endure. Though was busy with family & children, but still had that desire to do something in my life and for society.

But as you know, Everything doesn't seem right all the time. Time flew by and was then diagnosed with a health issue that caused a lot of pain to handle.

Doctors were unable to diagnose what happened... My husband and children were distraught!!

With so much pain in my body, One of my friends suggested Healing, and I went for the workshop with hope in my eyes and the result I got by the Grace of God was fantastic...

I was perfectly fine within a few days with no pain in my body and emotionally too I was feeling better.

I decided to learn more about healing and know the core of it.

This is how I started my journey.

'RISE BEYOND ORDINARY, HEAL BEYOND BODY!'

And today

I am a Healer/ Meditation coach/ Tarot card reader/Numerologist / Astrologer/Vastu expert.

I also learned a few more things that relate to yourself and your soul.

WRISTWATCH ANALYSIS

FACE DIAGNOSE AND TREATMENT.

SWITCH WORDS.

PLANETARY HEALING

BHAKTAMBAR HEALING.

ZIBU SYMBOLS

HEALING CORDS.

WATER THERAPY

MANIFESTATION

Worked in this field for the last 9 years and helped more than 5,000 people overcome their chronic issues such as depression, anxiety, hypertension, coma, and cancer.

I am blessed and thankful to GOD for making me the instrument of his DIVINE LOVE and LIGHT.

These modalities have changed my life and further here I am to bring changes in other people's Lives too.

In this book, I have tried to mention some common concerns and follow them with easy and beneficial remedies.

These remedies can heal you mentally and physically. An essential thing known as a remedy can change your entire life for good.

TABLE OF CONTENTS

INTRODUCTION 1

RITUALS THAT SHOULD BE FOLLOWED EVERY MONTH: 13

GENERAL VASTU TIPS 14

AUSPICIOUS PICTURES 17

AUSPICIOUS PLANTS ACCORDING TO DIRECTION 21

SIGNIFICANCE OF COLOUR AND REMEDIES . 25

VARIOUS FORMS OF GANPATI AS PER THE SITUATION - 30

DIWALI RITUALS 34

SAWAAN SPECIAL 37

AMAWASYA SPECIAL 40

HOW TO CONTROL OUR ANGER 41

RELATIONSHIPS 43

FINANCIAL TIPS 46

KUBER STONE 49

HEALTH ISSUES 51

SWITCH WORDS AND HEALING NUMBERS. ... 56

MEDITATION	61
SELF HEALING AFFIRMATION	63
NIGHT AFFIRMATION	64
AGGRESSIVE CHILDREN	65
GUPT NAVRATRI	66
WATER HEALING	71
WATER CODES	77
LIVING WATER	84
WATER TREATMENT	86
MONEY SHOWER RITUAL	89
TECHNIQUE "GLASS OF WATER"	95
SELF-TUNING	98
PRACTICE "MAGIC ELIXIR"	100

INTRODUCTION

Many of you might have this question

'WHY ONLY ME?'

'MERI HI LIFE ME ASA KYU HAI !'

'I HAVE DONE NOTHING WRONG NOR I HAVE CHEATED ANYONE!'

'NEITHER DO I TRY TO HURT ANYONE WITH MY WORDS OR ACTIONS.'

THEN WHY AM I HAVING ISSUES IN MY LIFE...

FEW PEOPLE WHO ARE VERY RUDE AND HAVE CHEATED A LOT STILL THEIR LIVES IS SO SMOOTH!!!!

WHY???

So the life that we have now is based on our karmas of what we have done in our last or in any of our incarnations... And according to that we have chosen our life...

Answer me, If you have 50 lakh in your pocket and you need to purchase a house can you purchase a home worth 1 crore..

No, I guess

You will search for the best house for you and your family which comes under your budget...

Right !!!!

So is the same with your life that you have been gifted by God.

The karma that you generated in your previous incarnation has inured the opportunity to choose your life/parents/ friends/ family and everything according to that and believe me you are the only one who has chosen the best option among all those which you deserved...

So the first thing is to stop complaining to others about what you are facing...

It's all our destiny, No one is responsible for circumstances in our lives.

And forgiving and forgiveness is the best key to unlocking all the closed doors in our lives.

If a person hurts us with their words or actions, believe me, most of the time they are suffering too.

Have you ever been scolded by your parents, teachers, or elder siblings?

Just close your eyes and ask yourself how many times till now?

I am sure you don't remember all the situations and just because you love them, you are emotionally attached to them.

Isn't it?

So why think about them with whom you are not connected? People come in and teach us a few lessons and go away. So why is the anger and aggression related to them still within?

Should you forgive them and move forward because they are not stuck but WE ARE?

Sometimes we are guilty and can't even forgive ourselves.

Let's face it, Our lives unfold based on how we think. The good news is that if we believe the right thoughts then life unfolds accordingly. The bad news is that if we consider the wrong thoughts, then life unfolds accordingly. Controlling our thoughts is one of the most challenging things we can do, because the mind, left to its device is like a drunk monkey sometimes, randomly jumping from one thought to the next. One thought makes us happy, another makes us sad, and another thought starts us worrying about something that only "might happen". It is pretty crazy sometimes. Do you know what your next thought is going to be? Not usually, it just shows up.

The good news is that whenever you are having complex thoughts that are non-productive and stressing you out, it is time to take control of your thoughts and focus on happier ones. This practice creates all those miracles that you can think of.

When I read about all the heartache and destruction in the world and take responsibility for becoming aware of that reality in my consciousness, I am very sorry. This realization can be difficult to accept, and our ego will resist this level of responsibility, but once you start practicing forgiveness you will see results are nothing less than miraculous.

A great exercise is to choose something that you already know you've caused for yourself.

Over-weight? Addicted to nicotine, alcohol, or some other substance? Do you have anger or self-esteem issues? Health problems? Start there and say you're sorry. Just say I'm SORRY. That's it! It is even more powerful to say it more clearly: "I realize that I am responsible for this (issue) in my life and I feel remorse that my consciousness has allowed this."

So before starting the journey let's have some insights about what remedy is. And how it works?

Lots of people might be performing a few rituals regularly and some may follow something for a couple of days or more as per their requirement but are remedies really powerful??

The answer is YES!!!

BUT BUT BUT

It's powerful only if your emotions are attached to it, if someone performs any ritual forcefully or unwantedly there is no use in doing anything and it will be just a waste of time and money as well.

In simple words, if I explain remedy is just like anaesthesia which is given to a patient before any major surgery..

What does anesthesia do?

It doesn't allow the patient to realize the pain or discomfort they will face...

In the same way, remedy works like anaesthesia which help us to overcome that period that is going to be critical in our life or even if our life is stuck somewhere.

Performing remedy is like training our subconscious mind that everything will be fine because our subconscious mind is mighty and attractive...

Isn't it amazing this is the fact that we attract those things or situations in our life that are going on within us and we are not aware of that?

Even if we start appreciating ourselves or start saying some positive words to ourselves, after a few days you will notice that we start growing in that way...

Like

I am blessed

I am happy

I am strong

I am powerful

And so on...

Even these simple words can change our and other's thought processes.

And you won't believe it but the best way to start our day is <u>GRATITUDE</u>...

GRATITUDE for everything around us because it is the state of being that allows us to see positive things around us .. as human beings we have a nature to constructively deal with negative situations rather than focusing on the positive.

Just like our tongue can be obsessed with something stuck in our teeth, our mind has a default setting just to focus on negativity all around.

Gratitude is a state that allows us to see the positivity around us and realize that there is good in the world.

Gratitude even graces us with inner strength and confidence that if we are blessed as human beings God has given us enough.

As human beings, we are blessed to see, hear, touch, feel, and do whatever we want to.. isn't it amazing?

And we are not too busy to be grateful.

Gratitude is not an emotion; it's a way of life that can be learned and practiced regularly.

WELL, Will discuss Gratitude more in some other book and now come back to the topic of remedy.

So when we perform any ritual or any special puja or remedy, we start developing a thought process that things will become better and everything will be fine...

AND SO, it starts happening in our life...

The remedy is something which is performed with faith, clear and pure intention... The results come into action...

We all know LORD HANUMAN JI went to search SANJIVANI for Lord Laksham because that was the only remedy to save his life then.

You all might have listened to or read in Indian mythology that all the demons used to perform a special puja for years and years to please God and when it was completed, they asked for blessings from the creator...

That was also a remedy they used to perform to fulfill their desires...

But we human beings are blessed that we don't have to travel like Hanunam ji nor do we have to perform yagya(yajna) or fire rituals for years and years.

In today's life, it's easy to perform and connect with the Divine but as I mentioned before, our mind has a default setting that focuses only on the negativity around us.

I have tried to mention in this book the maximum number of simple techniques which are easy to perform with good results.

But remember

GRATITUDE FOR EVERYTHING IS IMPORTANT.

KEEP YOUR INTENTIONS CLEAR AND SEE THE MAGIC

People knowingly or unknowingly perform space cleaning in their daily lives. Whitewashing, painting, arranging the furniture, cleaning the domestic objects and various such activities of keeping the house clean are nothing but some simple ways of space clearing and purifying.

These regular activities never allow the domestic energy to get stagnant or aged and thus fresh energy is constantly generated in the house.

Every individual should be aware of the energy in the house. Energy can be impaired by dirt, garbage, foul smell, and noise in the house. Dead objects like dry leaves and flowers generate negative energies. Special attention should be paid to the cleansing of exposed articles like curtains, bedsheets, carpets, window- panes, etc.

However, certain rituals can be followed once a month or more.

USE OF RAW SALT

The significance of salt is for taste in food. This salt is also used to avoid diseases. Bathing in warm salty water removes fatigue and brings freshness.

Salty water is capable of killing germs. Spraying it in the house can therefore prevent many diseases.

Raw salt from the sea is always used for the purification of the environment. Procured or iodized salt is available in the market and is never used for this process.

The floor of the house can be washed with a salt-water solution. 200gm raw salt is added to one liter of water.

USE OF AIR AND SUNLIGHT

Open and pure air is considered healthy. So doors and windows should be kept open for half an hour daily.

Sunlight is also responsible for energizing the environment. The sun is the primary source of energy for life on Earth. If a house has remained closed for a long time, sunlight is very important for the treatment of stagnant energy there.

All the doors, windows, and curtains should be opened in such a situation that light enters the house.

USE OF SOUND

Sounds are also used in the rituals of purification of the environment. Sounds affect a lot in our daily lives. Everything that exists has its sound. It means that besides living things, non-living things also have their sound. Every substance in the universe emits energy and also produces sound. This sound depends upon the energy surrounding those substances. Every sense has atoms. These atoms are in continuous motion. It is their speed that generates sound. Sound is straightforward and pleasing when there is coordination among the particles.

According to Indian beliefs, the creation of the universe was from the sound of "OM". Word is considered as "Brahma", the almighty in India. This is a kind of energy, which never perishes. Spoken by us, get embedded in the vast universe. Thus sound has been given respect and importance since the ancient period.

BELLS, CYMBALS, VEDIC MANTRAS, MUSIC, ETC. are used to purify the environment through sound.

Wind chimes at the entrance or any corner of shops prevent the negative energies of that place.

Cymbals should be played three times at the entrance of the house. After this, it should be played thrice in every corner, clockwise in every room.

This process can be done by a Bell.

Soft music in the evening will relieve one from the fatigue and stress of a busy day. Good music will always have a good effect. Thus, positive energies will persist in the house if holy and pleasant music waves run through it. Music will have a miraculously positive impact in an environment of discord and woe in a house. It will always protect against negative thoughts. Care should however be taken to play music only at a comfortable low volume. High-pitched and loud music may cause harm on the contrary.

Music therapy is now being used in the treatment of diseases. Music is helpful in meditation also. Soft music in the room helps concentration in studies too.

USE OF CHANTS

Chanting religious hymns accompanied by aromatized smoke of incense is yet another way of purifying the space. Chants from Veda, Purana, and other spiritual ancient texts are recited at houses. Also reading RAMAYANA or BHAGWAT GITA brings positive energies into the house. These especially synchronize well with singing bowls or music bells.

Chants and prayers produce the sound of a definite frequency. This sound helps clean and purify the environment. The chant "OM" is sung with incense sticks and aromatized smoke, the chant rises with the smoke and purifies the whole room. This is a very powerful chanting.

USE OF LIGHT

Light is considered auspicious in every civilization. Oil and ghee lamps are lighted on various religious occasions. Light is used where there is an increase of "dull energy" in the house.

Oil lamps remove negativity from life while ghee lamp brings positivity. If a person is facing any problems then he must light an oil Deepak(lamp) in the temple. Similarly for improvement, one should use a ghee lamp.

RITUALS THAT SHOULD BE FOLLOWED EVERY MONTH:

1) On the first date of the month, take a tablespoon of cinnamon into the palm of your hand, step outside of your front door, leave the front door open, and blow the cinnamon into your home, over your doorway. As you do so, think positive thoughts of abundance. You can even cast a spell or speak a mantra before you blow.

2) On every new moon and full moon (Amavasya and Purnima) donate rice, and milk, and make kheer in the temple.

3) On every Surya Sakranti (it occurs mid of every month) i.e. when Surya changes its rashi, offer seasonal fruit or food in the temple or Bharman.

GENERAL VASTU TIPS

One should donate one-sixth or ten percent of net profit to charity. This would give prosperity, expansion in income, and business success.

Bhagwat Gita describes what charity is and what are its benefits. According to Gita, charity gives to a worthy person simply because it is right to give, without consideration of anything in return, at the proper time and in the proper place, which is stated to be in the mode of goodness. From the wealth, you have earned by rightful means, take out one-tenth, and as a matter of duty, give it away in charity. Dedicate your charity for the pleasure of GOD.

Tithing removes karmic blocks that have stood in their way. The spiritual law of tithing says if you have that much to give that means you are open to receive more. Thus, tithing gives prosperity, name-fame, and success. But charity should be done carefully and one shouldn't be a victim of fraud in the name of charity.

1) Hanging horseshoes facing upward in a "U" shape is said to keep evil out and bring good luck into your home. Horseshoe is made of iron and iron is signified by Saturn. Moreover, the Horseshoe of a black horse works better if it is old which means that some black horse must have worn it some and has got worn out. Hanging

horseshoes pacifies the affliction of Saturn. Thus, hanging horseshoe as a remedy gives happiness, peace, and tranquility.

2) If the main door is in the wrong direction, put a convex mirror or a big plain mirror on the top of the door frame outside.

3) The septic tank should not be under the main door.

4) The Staircase should not face the main door. It drains energy. If it is so then place plants on every staircase (sidewise)

5) To protect from negative energies put TRI YANTRA (OM SWASTIK AND TRISHUL) on the main door facing outward.

6) The Toilet should not be to the side, or top, or opposite to the main door.

If it is so place the cactus plant in between the main door and the toilet's door as the cactus disintegrates dirty energy.

Put mirror/ convex mirror inside the toilet, on the wall which reflects the door.

7) Place two windows up on both sides of the main entrance.

It brings opportunities.

8) If a person/ profession/home/shop/ office is under the influence of the evil eye of someone, then bring an

iron nail to rotate 11 times from head to toe (if any takes take this nail to every corner of the anti-clockwise 11 times) and hammer it in the root of the wild fig tree (glooar). The evil effect will go away.

PICTURE AND ART PIECES

An inauspicious picture that creates mental as well as physical disturbance.

1) Picture of Ramayan, Mahabharat, a picture depicting war.

2) Picture of Gandharva (Demi-God), Naag (snake), and Apsaras (Fairies).

3) Pictures of phantoms, crying children, men or women are also unsuitable.

4) Pictures of injured, burnt, insane, idiots, and nudes should also be avoided.

5) picture of hunting and jungle fire.

6) Pictures of thorny plants, dry flowers, and naked trees should also not be displayed.

7) Pictures of bore, fox, buffalo, crow, eagle, and such birds must be avoided.

8) Pictures of God and Goddesses should also not be used for decoration.

9) Pictures that generate feelings of fear, anger, or any such thing should also be avoided.

AUSPICIOUS PICTURES

1· Swastik

It is drawn before starting anything so that the work is completed without any problem. Swastik is drawn on both sides of the house entrance.

Swastik means welfare or auspicious. It is taken also in the sense of welfare, blessings, virtue, and destroyer of sins.

2· OM

OM in Indian culture is accepted as a form of Brahma. This entire cosmos was born out of Om. Formless Brahma and ultimate power are the form of OM.

3· KALASH

Kalash filled with water and decorated with mango and banana leaves and flowers was considered a symbol of auspiciousness, prosperity, and affluence. Water is a must for life. In nature firth living beings emerged in water. This fact has a scientific base also. Indian religious texts say that God's first incarnation was Matsyavatar i.e. fish was accepted as the first incarnation. That is why before installing Kalash it is filled with water. Mango has been accepted as an evergreen and pious tree. In havan also mango wood is used. Mango leaves are a symbol of life and its continuity. Coconut is also very important in dev Puja. In all religious rituals, auspicious ceremonies, festivity, etc. Mangal Kalash is installed in the house. While worshipping the kalash water of all holy rivers is invited. Thereafter only any religion or auspicious work begins. Not only in houses but in temples also this pious symbol is engraved. Kalash can be seen in the domes of the temple. It is drawn on the walls of the house. It brings happiness, prosperity, and affluence.

4· FISH

Fish is taken to be an auspicious being. The first incarnation came in the form of fish. Many people look at the fish before proceeding on a journey. Many people draw fish on both sides of the main door of the house. Fish is the symbol on Kamdev's flag. Also, the shape of fish in many ornaments is very popular. Painting a Fish couple at the door or wall of the house is auspicious.

5· PANCHAGULAK HAND (PALM)

This too is a traditional auspicious symbol. Impression palms on both sides of the main door entrance on the occasion of marriage, housewarming, childbirth, and other such happenings are observed. The lady of the house does this.

Turmeric paste is prepared and its palm impression is made. These impressions are five in number. The hand is a symbol of action (karma). God's assuring posture (the abhay mudra) and blessing posture are of hands palm.

The impression of a hand in the house brings happiness and prosperity. It also highlights the importance of karma.

6- The Presiding deity's (clan deity of the family) picture should be more than 12 inches long.

7- On both sides of the entrance door watchmen should be in good attire and wearing jewellery holding a sword and welcome. With each Watchmen there should be a watch woman also.

8- Lakshmi's seat on the Lotus, being sprinkled with a white elephant is considered very auspicious.

9 - The Cow with net calf beautifully painted or exposed is good.

10- A Picture of women singing and dancing is preferable.

11- Picture or statue of a parrot, peacock, or swan bird that pleases the eyes.

12- Pictures of the garden are refreshing.

13- A Picture of Kuber Yantra in the North direction is also worth displaying.

14- A Picture of water bodies, full of water birds and tanks blooming with Lotus flowers in the Northeast of the house is auspicious.

15- A Picture of any season exhibition with eye-catching scenery is always good.

16- Picture of inspiring great men and heroes.

AUSPICIOUS PLANTS ACCORDING TO DIRECTION

NORTH EAST
Tulsi

Tulsi is also a healing plant and can be kept in the room of the patient.

Bamboo

Zed (Trasula)

Golden furn

Fish lily

Presth city

Orkut

Ipomoea green

EAST
Sunflower

Palm tree

Peony

Jasmine

Arica palm tree

Fitonia

Chrysanthemum

SOUTH
Ficus (black/green)
Bromeliad
Peperomia
ZZ plant
Fig

SOUTH EAST
Agleomena lipstick Red
Marble leaf money plant
Oxalis
Croton red
Tropical Hibiscus
Caladium pink

SOUTH WEST
Snake plant
Spider plant
Dracena plant
Dragon plant
White bird of paradise

WEST
Neem
Touch me not
Yucca cane

Raphis palm
Cactus
Pointed succulence

NORTH
Purple Queen
Rhoeo spathacea
Green leaf money plant
Golden leaf money plant
Heart leaf money plant
Aprajita

NORTH WEST
Agleomena lipstick white
String of pearls
Air plant
Pandanus
Dracaena

CENTRE
Table palm
Prayer plant
Tulsi (Holi basil)
Plum blossom

INAUSPICIOUS PLANT FOR RESIDENCE.

Pakar plant

Neem tree

Peepal tree

Vair tree

Imli tree

Pomegranate (South East direction is preferable)

Bel

Date palm

Gular tree (South is preferable but if in North give trouble to eyes).

These leaf plants are not good as they create fear from the enemy.

Any plant that releases milk is not auspicious as it creates financial losses.

SIGNIFICANCE OF COLOUR AND REMEDIES

Colour affects moods, personality, feelings, and physical energy.

When exposed to different colour vibrations, human is known to experience changes in their mental, emotional, and physical state. The choice of colour depends on person to person. Some people might like a particular colour whereas might repel against some colour.

Sunlight consists of seven colours of the rainbow. Every colour has vibrations and they travel in different frequencies. According to studies, colour when transmitted from the eye to the brain, the brain releases a hormone affecting emotions, mind clarity, and energy levels. The negative and positive psychological effects of colour can be observed in human beings based on the combination in which they are used.

If we can recognize an appropriate colour that involves the feeling of happiness and pleasure, we can use such colours in our surroundings to keep ourselves positive all the time.

The colour therapist suggests a certain combination of colours for occasions, events, marriages, birthday parties, etc. which gives happiness to the guests. Using auspicious colours expands the personality of the person.

Auspicious colour according to numerologists can be derived from the date of birth, i.e. the day, month, and year.

The colour signified by the total number derived would be the auspicious colour to the native.

Auspicious colours expand comfort, prosperity, and happiness.

It is not necessary to use lucky colours only in the form of wearing that particular colour of clothes. One can use lucky colours in the office/ home in the form of accessories such as pens, paper, socks, handkerchiefs, wall colours, etc.

Lucky colour brings favourable surroundings and brings positive energy.

Using lucky colours in various rooms of the house can enhance peace, happiness, compatibility, tranquility, etc. in the environment of the home.

The colour representing the planet which is strong and favourable in the native's chart can be used in bedsheets, curtains, wall paint, etc.

This shall enhance prosperity, fame, and wellness.

The red colour is believed to give excitement, and aggression whereas the Orange and Yellow colours give hope and happiness. They all are said to be warm colours and are bright by nature. On the other hand, Blue and

Green are cool colour and bring peace to the mind, Whereas Black and Brown is signified by Saturn and Rahu, thus excessive use of these colours might amplify the effect of Saturn and Rahu, as a result, the person might be prone to stress and anxiety.

White colour on the other hand increases ambition and receptivity.

Here is the list of planets and colours associated with each other.

SUN- ORANGE, YELLOW, GOLDEN SHADES, AND TINTS.

MOON- YELLOW, SILVER, PEARL WHITE, OLIVE GREEN

MARS- RED, CRIMSON, PINK, MAROON.

MERCURY- GREEN

JUPITER - YELLOW, LEMON YELLOW, GOLDEN

VENUS- NAVY BLUE, SKY BLUE, SHINY AND BRIGHT COLOUR.

SATURN- BLACK, DARK BLUE, DARK BROWN.

KETU- OCEAN BLUE COLOUR, MAUVE, LAVENDER, GREY, BLACK, AND WHITE PEARL.

RAHU- SMOKEY BLUE COLOUR, GREY, BROWN.

NOTE: There is a general theory that cruel and malefic planets signify dark colours whereas light colours are represented by benefit planets.

<u>Zodiac sign and colour</u>

The selection of colour should be determined by the native's ascendant or moon sign. It is better to determine whether the ascendant or moon sign is stronger and thus the colour representing a stronger sign should be selected.

According to some scholars, the colour representing the Ascendant or Moon sign during the auspicious time of housewarming can also be selected.

ZODIAC SIGN AND COLOUR

ARIES- ALL SHADES OF RED

TAURUS -MILKY WHITE

GEMINI - ALL SHADES AND TINTS OF GREEN

CANCER - LIGHT PINK AND PEARL WHITE

LEO - LIGHT YELLOW, CREAM, AND ORANGE

VIRGO- LIGHT GREEN, SKY BLUE.

LIBRA - WHITE, GREY, BEIGE, MULTICOLOUR

SCORPIO - RED, BRIGHT PINK, COPPER

SAGITTARIUS - GOLDEN YELLOW, GOLDEN

CAPRICORN - ALL SHADES OF BLUE, BROWN

AQUARIUS - BLUE, LIGHT PINK, BLACK

PISCES - WHITE, YELLOW, DULL YELLOW, MUSTARD.

VARIOUS FORMS OF GANPATI AS PER THE SITUATION -

People in India believe a lot in worshipping and it's good to do. A ritual that is seen commonly in Indian houses is the Ganpati idol at the main entrance. There are various forms of Lord Ganesh here I am discussing a few of them to give a clear idea of which idol of GANESHA to install in different situations.

SANTAAN GANPATI (Ganpati in a child form)

The idol of GANESHA in child form is kept at the entrance door for overcoming progeny issues. The childless couple with utmost faith should worship the idol and install it in the home at a perfect mahurat.

VIGHNAHARTA GANPATI -

In a house where there is always a situation of distress, misery, obstacles, mental agony, etc........ In such a house, VIGHNAHARTA GANPATI should be installed at the entrance door and witness the magic. In Vighnaharta Ganesha idol is infused with two mantras,

1- Nirhanyay Namah

2- Avighnyay Namah

VIDYAPRADAYAK GANPATI -

In houses where children are notorious and in-disciplined and are not interested in studies or they can't memorize their studies etc. In such a house, the VIDYAPRADAYAK GANPATI idol should be installed at the entrance door in an auspicious mahurat. The idol should be infused with Mantra such as

1- Gyanrupaya Namah

2- Vidyaniharya Namah

3- Vidyadhanya Namah

4- Gyanmudravate Namah

VIVAH VINAYAK GANPATI

In many houses, girls or boys with a certain marriage age do not get an appropriate alliance. Mostly, they have obstacles in marriage due to the ill effects of Mars in their chart. In such a case, Vivah Vinayak Ganpati should be installed at the entrance of the door at the appropriate Mahurat.

The idol should be invoked with Mantras;

1) Kamnikantkarshya Namah

2) Sakalkampradayak Namah

3) Kamdayay Namah.

DHANDAYAK GANPATI

At present, life is incomplete and relatively worthless without money. It is extremely difficult to have materialistic pleasure without wealth. In some houses, there is always a lack of wealth even though the natives or other members work hard to earn it. There is a lack of prosperity and thus money earned goes away easily or is spent in undesirable situations.

In such houses, DHANDAYAK GANPATI should be installed at the entrance door and should be invoked with Mantra such as;

1) Shripatye Namah

2) Mahalaxmi Priyatama Namah

3) Sidhi Laxmi Manoharpraya Namah

4) Koti dheeshvarai Namah.

SIDDHIVINAYAK GANPATI

It should be installed for the manifestation of success in every work and situation. The idol of Siddhivinayak Ganpati should be installed at the entrance and should be invoked with Mantras;

1) Siddhvyaya Namah

2) Siddhivinayakyay Namah

3) Ridhi - Sidhi Pradaykayay Namah

RIN MOCHAN GANPATI

Rin mochan Ganpati should be installed when the native is not able to get rid of the loan and is overlapping day by day. The idol should be infused with Mantra;

1) Rintraya Vimochanayay Namah and install the idol in PUSHAYA NAKSHATRA.

DIWALI RITUALS

1) Bring mud (Pili Mitti) on Dhanteras at auspicious times and keep it at your Puja place.. or you can spread it on your Puja ground.

It is the symbol of prosperity!

2) If a person writes the following yantra with a **pomegranate** pen and **ashwagandha** ink and worships the yantra on the occasion of Deepavali and keeps it in his safe then he will never have financial difficulties.

The yantra is to be written on the leaf and bark of the Himalayan birch tree (Bhoj Patra) facing east. While writing the person must have cardamom (elaichi) in his mouth and he should sit on a mat of wool. While writing first make 16 squares. Then write the numbers in each square where it should be and begin with no 1.

On Deepavali night make this yantra and perform its Puja with Lakshmi Puja. The power of the yantra gets increased by following the above rules.

16	6	4	5
3	6	15	10
13	12	1	8
2	7	14	11

3) For stable Lakshmi...

Take one iron utensil, put water add sugar, milk, and ghee in it. Stand below the peepal tree and pour the entire mixture into the roots of the peepal tree...

And pray to maa Lakshmi.

4) Take a beautiful mud pot, keep some silver item/ coin or gold coin or regular 5-10 rs coin covered by red colour cloth in that pot, fill the entire pot with rice or wheat and keep it in the Northwest corner of your house.

5) On Deepavali, one should light four sided Deepak (4 mukhi) in all the corners of the house/shop. And pray to LORD GANESHA for good health and wealth.

6) To seek the blessings of maa Lakshmi, burn elaichi and clove (laung) together, make the powder, and offer to all the devi and devatas in your house temple especially to maa Lakshmi.

7) If you are facing a problem with your job start with the AMAWASYA of DEEPAVALI offers sweet rice to crows every day till you get the desired job.

8) If you get troubled by your enemy.. on Deepavali's night, take a blank paper write the name of your enemy with kajal made with Kapur, and rub it with your leg.

9) For a healthy relationship, offer kheer to maa Lakshmi and then offer the Prasad to everyone in the family.

10) Offer Lotus flower and Nariyal in Maa Lakshmi temple on Deepavali and it will open all the doors of abundance in your life.

SAWAAN SPECIAL

Sawaan is a beautiful month in the entire year. A month when Mother Earth is standing with open arms, as greenery is all around with different and beautiful flowers blooming. A month of spirituality, a month to heal ourselves mentally emotionally, and physically.

There is a ritual that is followed from year and year i.e. offering water, milk, etc. to LORD SHIVA.. As it is believed that Shiva is a deity who has the power to heal you in all aspects of life.

When we offer water to lord Shiva we get healed emotionally, which is very much important.

If you carefully see or examine our pineal gland, it is shaped like a Shiv Ling. And our pineal gland runs our whole body as Shiv runs the whole Universe.

Hormones which are produced by the pineal gland plays an important part in our body as same as worshipping Lord Shiva in the month of Sawan plays an important role in our life.

It also teaches us to forgive and forget who is our enemy and be with them as oneness.

Lord Shiva has a snake on his neck and his son Kartikey rides on a Peacock, as both snake and Peacock are enemies of each other but still if you observe they are at the same place in every temple.

This could be the greatest example and learning to be kind and generous.

It also helps to unblock our Heart Chakra and the flow of love and peace energy within us enhances.

Rituals that can be followed during Sawan are mentioned below you can choose any one or multiple.

a) One should wake up before sunrise. This should be practiced regularly, if not possible at least in Sawan month, waking up before sunrise is like activating all your Planets.

b) People in Government jobs should offer water mixed with rose water to the Sun and should chant Om mentally.

c) SHIV PUJA (offering water, milk, honey, etc.) should be done entire Sawan.

d) Avoid wearing black or blue colour throughout Sawan.

(The concept of colours I have already explained in another chapter)

e) If you face many health challenges, you can chant HANUMAN CHALISA in front of the Sun.

f) Write your wish on yellow paper with a red pen, and show it to Surya Dev daily. Just say "Thank you Surya Dev for fulfilling my wishes".

Note: your wish should be very practical.

g) Feed animals with milk, biscuits, and other dairy products every day.

h) Donate sleepers, clothes, food etc to Brahmins.

i) Specially for Government jobs, offer gud (jaggery), Chapatti to red cow or any other cow. After offering they should take 7 rounds around the cow.

AMAWASYA SPECIAL

Amawasya is day for our ancester. Amawas is considered a very powerful day to do black magic or to perform such activities, also this day is very powerful to perform a few rituals that may help you to get rid of many difficulties you are facing in your life like healing challenges, financial setbacks, evil eye, etc.

These rituals can be performed for any problem you are facing, the only thing is your intention and the result you want should be clear in your mind.

a) Offer a small packet/ box of saffron to Maa Lakshmi, leave it overnight and the next day of amawas after your daily Puja routine take that box and keep it in your locker.

b) For positivity in your house, wash your floor on every amawas and make rangoli.

c) Make a 4-sided Deepak with wheat flour, use mustard oil to light it, and keep it in your South direction.

Don't forget to remember your ancestors (Pitra dev).

d) Offer white flowers to pictures of your ancestors.

e) Donate white things.

Kheer is best to donate on Amawas.

f) You can feed cows, and dogs on this day.

HOW TO CONTROL OUR ANGER

When I read about all the heartache and destruction in the world and take responsibility for becoming aware of that reality in my consciousness, I am very sorry. This realization can be difficult to accept, and our ego will resist this level of responsibility, once you start practicing forgiveness, you will see results that are nothing less than miracles.

A great exercise is to choose something that you already know you've caused for yourself. Over-weight? Addicted to nicotine, alcohol, or some other substance? Do you have anger or self-esteem issues? Health problems? Start there and say you're sorry. Just say I'm SORRY. That's it! It is even more powerful to say it more clearly: "I realize that I am responsible for this (issue) in my life and I feel remorse that my consciousness has allowed this.

SIMPLE 3 STEPS that you need to remember in life -

1 - Acknowledge

2 - Conversation

3 - Release

1. ACKNOWLEDGE

Witness the fact that you are angry. Accept it and tell yourself that it's normal:) Acknowledge that you are angry.

2. CONVERSATION

Have a conversation with the Universe.

Dear Universe,

I am unaware of what's inside me that's creating this experience.

Allow me to transmute this experience into love and light.

3. RELEASE

Start saying four phrases that will release your anger -

I LOVE MYSELF

I AM SORRY TO HURT MYSELF FORGIVE ME THANK YOU!

Keep repeating them till your anger vanishes:)

RELATIONSHIPS

Relationships are an essential aspect of human life, contributing to our emotional well-being, personal growth, and social connections. They can be complex and require communication, trust, respect, and effort from all parties involved to thrive and maintain a healthy balance.

1) Store rainwater in a silver bottle or glass bottle and keep it in the northwest direction.

2) Clean waste, and leather unwanted items from your cupboard and house especially all the corners it enhances Saturn energy there.

3) Keep your terrace clean.

4) For arguments between couples, mix 250 gm of rice with 150 gm of green dal and keep it in your bedroom.

5) Make bread cutlets on Friday and try to have your meal together, it helps in better understanding and generates love and respect.

6) Avoid Roman number watches in your bedroom, as Roman numbers attract strangers.

7) Avoid having too much black colour (pink is preferable for the bedroom) as black makes your partner very specific and choosy.

8) Draw this symbol on white paper with a blue pen and stick it on your bedroom door, cupboard, or wall.

It helps generate good relationships and love between couples.

You can use this symbol in your child's room too.

9) Don't keep your head in the East direction while sleeping it may manifest health challenges.

10) If your child is not under your instructions. Father should gift him/ her a pair of shoes on Sunday.

But generally, we should avoid purchasing shoes on Sunday as Sunday has the Sun's energy, and shoes are connected with Saturn.

11) A person who keeps mango saplings on his arms or neck becomes happy. Provided that the sapling was plucked during the Uttra Falguni Constellation.

FOR GETTING MARRIAGE

If a girl's marriage is not getting fixed, she is advised to take a five-coloured thread, equal to her height or double her height. Then she must tie 80 (eighty) turmeric knots at equal distances and thus make a sort of chain. She must then go to LORD GANESH TEMPLE with 89 (eighty-nine) dates, there she should put the chain of turmeric and 9 (nine) dates at the feet of Lord GANESHA and bring back 80(eighty) dates. She must then eat one date (kajoor) regularly. By the grace of LORD GANESHA, her marriage will be fixed.

FINANCIAL TIPS

Money is something that is very important to survive in this physical World.

A few rituals to be done on Diwali that I have explained in another chapter.

Here are a few general tips that can be performed any day and will help you overcome your financial issues.

1) Take small Nariyal, Gomti chakra, yellow Kodee, Shangk, and pearl (moti). Tie all these in red colour cloth and keep it in your cash box after prayer.

2) Keep SHRI YANTRA

in your cash box or house temple, make sure that you worship it daily.

3) Donate rice on every Purnima(full moon) for financial gain.

4) Never gift roasted almonds on Wednesday to anyone, it brings financial loss.

5) Cut ginger (Adarak) into a star shape, 3 piece keep it outside the door on the right-hand side, and let the sweeper swipe it the next day. Continue it for the next forty (40) days. Your stopped/ blocked work will come in progress.

6) Keep 5 Lotus stalks with 5 Tumeric pieces in a safe/ locker, it brings wealth and money.

7) Pluck one peepal leaf on Saturday and bring it to your office/ shop, keep it safe. Bring another leaf next Saturday, when 7 leaves accumulate then immerse them into a well or river.

8) Take a few papaya seeds, dry them up, and sew these seeds in black cloth or string and tie them on your arms or the main door of your office/shop/ home.

It will protect from black magic and evil eyes.

9) Keeping 5 knobs of turmeric and 11 Lotus buts duly packed in a safe, the person goes richer and richer.

10) Bring roots of a Banyan tree in the Pushya Constellation. Note, that the root should be from deep touching the ground. Then keeping it in the locker increases wealth. You can chant Gayatri Mantra 27 or 108 times which will be more auspicious.

11) If the sapling of mango is taken during Ravi Pushya yoga and kept in the pocket then the native wins over all his adversaries.

12) Place a figure of an Owl in the locker or cupboard where you keep your money.

13) Pray to Goddess Lakshmi on Fridays and light 9 ghee lamps.

14) Place a Vastu Aishwarya Lakshmi photo at the front door or in the northeast direction.

15) Fix the Siddha Vyapaar Vriddhi Yantra in your business place at an auspicious time , make sure that you make part of your prayers before.

16) Keep a small hand mirror in your locker. Clean it every time you look at it.

17) Donate toys to orphaned children.

KUBER STONE

Bring home this Kuber stone for an overflow of abundance and eliminate stress from your lives. Kuber stone is a 400+ million-year-old fossil and thus a powerful 'stone' with the absorption of cosmic energies over time.

✤ Healing properties of Kuber Stone are :

- The Kuber stone stores very powerful Earth energies and that's why it is very effective in clearing and balancing the root chakra.

- It provides you with the much-needed grounding and supporting energies.

- The Kuber stone is very influential for business, career, and financial abundance.

- The fossils in the stone increases the life span, alleviate stress, and anxiety, reduce toxins, maintain emotional stability, and make the person more confident.

HEALTH ISSUES

Health is the biggest wealth.. if we are fit, we are blessed to do whatever we want to. But if not ...

Life just stops...

So I am sharing a few tips that are safe and don't harm us for different health challenges.

because taking medicines is like curing one issue and giving invitations to many more.

In the next chapter, I have shared a few healing cords and switch words and have discussed more in that chapter.

BUT

Here are some common HEALTH ISSUES and their REMEDIES -

STONE

a) Consumption of 2 spoon full of Ashoka seed powder with water regularly for a few days to cure stone-related issues.

b) By taking Ash of Margosa (neem) leaf with Luke warm water regularly stone or lithe in the kidney is broken and its particles are flushed out with urine.

c) Hibiscus flower powder one tablet spoon with lukewarm water every night before going to bed cures stone-related problems.

(should not have anything after this)

d) Drinking radish carrot juice 1/2 a cup daily helps to cure the stone issue within a week.

e) Drinking wheat grass juice daily morning an empty stomach helps in the reduction of a stone.

BLISTERS AND ULCER

a) For a blister in the mouth, have a banana with curd made of cow's milk for continues 7- 10 days.

b) Make a decoction of Jasmine leaves and gargle twice a day. This cures blisters and also works on gum disease.

c) Make a juice of java plum (jamun) leaf. Gargling with this cures mouth boils and even the bad smell in breath disappears if done regularly for a few days.

d) Chewing Jasmine leaves is also effective in toothache and mouth blister.

e) Dry up mango leaves and make Ash by burning them, rub this Ash with a pinch of salt on the teeth for a few seconds, this will protect the teeth from disease and make them stronger.

f) Use of Margosa (Neem) and Datun (teeth cleaning twig) as toothbrushes is very good for teeth.

ASTHAMA

a) Asthmatic patients are advised to take 30-40 drops of Margosa (neem) seed oil in water.

If taken empty stomach then it is more effective.

Neem seed oil is easily available in stores.

b) Drill a small hole in a ripe banana, stuff it with black pepper, and keep it in the open during the night. In the morning roast it on a mild flame, and chew it with black pepper as well. It helps in curing Asthma attacks.

JOINT PAIN

Boil white Oak root in sesame oil thoroughly. Then have a gentle massage on the affected part, regular application and soft massage reduce the pain.

b) Apply sweet oil or ghee on Oak leaves, heat them slightly, and tie them on the affected part. It helps reduce pain.

Ghee works better in this case.

HEADACHE

a) Juice of java plum (jamun) leaf is a wonder for headache.

b) In approximately, 1 litre of sesame oil mix 5 elements of Lotus (flower, stem, root, leaf, and kesar). Boil it thoroughly, then filter it. The application of this oil on the head reduces headaches, and tension, and the person feels soothing and cool.

c) Three Jasmine flowers should be ground with Gul Rogan oil and may be dropped in the nostrils. The headache will subside.

GAS AND ACIDITY

a) Pain caused by gas subsides, take a spoonful of Ashwagandha powder with a cup of milk every morning and evening for a few days.

b) Having 3 drops of Badam Rogan oil with Luke's warm milk on an empty stomach helps in curing Acidity issues.

c) Take half a cup of warm water, mix one teaspoon of Ghee with a pinch of salt, and drink it empty stomach for 4-5 days. It helps in curing chronic Acidity problems.

d) By taking a small quantity of peepal leaf every morning empty stomach and Chewing it properly cure many body problems. The resistance power of the body increases.

e) 3 gram turmeric powder and a pinch of salt, dissolved in water. Drinking this solution cures ulcers and acidity.

PILES

a) Make a powder of Pomegranate and brown sugar and let it dry for a few days. (example:100 Jaggery and 50 gram pomegranate powder). Take one spoon three times a day. This will cure piles, diarrhea , and indigestion.

b) Application of papaya milk on the warts of piles drives them quickly.

c) Take soft tendrils of mango, grind them in water, and drink, you can add some sugar for taste. Repeat this remedy every morning and evening till you get relief.

d) Make the powder of Pomegranate bark, one teaspoon of this powder with water if taken three times a day, helps in curing bloody piles.

DIABETES

a) Take leaves of java plum (Jamun) dry it and make fine powder, take one spoon every morning empty stomach, it helps in controlling diabetes.

SWITCH WORDS AND HEALING NUMBERS.

Switchwords were first identified by "Sigmund Freud". He suggested that certain words have the power to reach into and alter our subconscious.

This idea was seized upon by an Author, James T Mangan, who wrote his book "The Secret of Perfect Living". So he is the main contributor of giving this knowledge to the World.

Then Shunyam Nirav researched this concept further and came up with his book "Switchwords Easily Give to you whatever you want in life"

Switchwords are a string or combination of words that when combined together create new vibrations and the sound released by it slowly makes the difference.

Numbers again play an important role in our lives everything seems to start with a number and ends with a number. The nine planets, 12 zodiac signs, our date of birth, how much we earn? And a lot more .

Every calculation is based on numbers 0 to 9 .

These numbers have its own vibration and unique property, and when these are combined with each other it creates miracle.

In this chapter, I am going to share few numbers and Switchwords which are proven to be very powerful and effective.

You just need to chant these or write it down in a notebook at least 28 times daily for 43 days. Chanting can be done without counting.

For better result you can write this cords on your left hand with blue pen.

Please chant every number one by one and if space is given please respect that.

Few issues have more than one healing cord.

You can use both or only one as per your wish and believe.

Success - 2190

Promotion - 307410831

Progress - 318798

Blessed future - 22 18 609

Remove obstacles - 91688

Blocked money -520/ 897

Attract prosperity - 79

Miracle - 4418/1913

Everything is possible -777/741

Arthritis - 551 / 8111110

Back pain- 498217218227

Knee pain- 58 / 192493820

Insomnia - 8142543/ 531

Sleep disorder - 7048932

Constipation - 1501

Diarrhea - 557/ 45 45 899 / 584321

Vomiting - 1454215

Stomach discomfort - 62139

Stomach ache - 13 45 899

Bloating - 38 37 684

Diabetic -22574/ 8819977/512 1111

Hair fall - 5484121/ 22761097

Dental problem - 2914

Toothache - 5182544

Gum inflammation - 52088

Tonsillitis- 696

Thyroid gland - 67

Hypothyroidism - 1966

High BP - 88 63 292

Blood pressure - 814 6432

SWITCHWORDS

Switchwords can be used alone as well as with healing number cords.

- **To sell block property**

SPEED- COUNT - Hotcakes -ALLOW - BREAKTHROUGH - YES !

CRESCENDO - CONTINUE - Divine - ORDER - DROP - OIL - MIRACLE.

- **For easy work and success**

ELATE- AMAZING - BAMBOO -OIL -WINFALL- BONUS.

MAGIC CARPET - FULL- HAVEN- JEWEL- DAWN- ADD- MIRACLE.

- **For numb pain use**

ICE CUBE

or

CHANGE - ADJUST - ICE CUBE - WITH- Ice Blue.

- **To cut cords with any person/ though/ feeling**

CUT - CUT - CUT

or

CUT - DETACH - END.

- **Fast learning and doing well in exam**.

GENIUS - Qualified - REACH- CARE - JUDGE.

or

FATHOM- GENIUS - SLOW - CARE- REACH - Qualified - JUDGE.

- **Weights gain**

ADD- PUT- ON - BRICKS.

- **To attract clients and crack the deal**

RIDICULOUS - HOLD- GIVE- BOOM- MAGIC- COUNT - FLOW - TAP.

or

BUZZ- DO- FINALLY - DONE- CRACKER JACK.

MEDITATION

Meditation originally was meant to help deepen understanding of the sacred and mystical forces of life. Meditation is considered a type of mind-body complementary medicine. Meditation can produce a deep state of relaxation and a tranquil mind. The term "meditation" refers to a variety of practices that focus on mind and body integration and are used to calm the mind and enhance overall well-being.

Meditation is just simple deep breathing..

Deep inhale and deep exhale.

Inhale till 6 count deep through your abdomen hold for 3 counts and exhale for 6 count and again hold for 3 count.

The process is basically 6-3-6-3.

With tongue to your palette, it's helps you to connect easily with the higher energies, so

Being aware with your breathing helps you to solve lots of emotional and mental issues.

It help you to protect from negative thoughts.

Shield you from dirty, psychic energy.

It's helps you to remove negative thoughts and control energies like anger, stress. It's teaches you to let go .

Even meditation helps us to know better about our own self, it make us aware where we are wrong by criticizing or laughing on self, how sometimes we create negative energies looking on others good thing.

Sometimes we get effected, irritated, frustrated because of others, or we can say that we alone are not the victim(like COVID). But definitely we suffer.

Black magic done by using doll, picture of clothes can also be protected through meditation coz meditation makes our aura strong.

And to strengthen our aura we need to be spiritually developed which is easy to achieve through meditation.

SELF HEALING AFFIRMATION

To the supreme being, flood me with your healing and purifying light.

I forgive all those who have caused me injury or pain.

I release all the hurts. I am at peace and filled with love. My whole being is becoming healthier and healthier every day.

In every way, I am getting better and better.

God is Merciful, God is Almighty. He is healing me if all my ailments, in full faith and in Deep Gratitude.

As I wish

So be it.

Take few deep breathe and relax.

NIGHT AFFIRMATION

The past is over and finished,

I AM FREE

I have a new feeling of pride and courage.

I have confidence in my ability to love and of being self sufficient.

I have learned that I am capable of growing and to change positivety.

I AM STRONG

I am in union with the whole of life in unity with the power and intelligence of the universe.

DIVINE wisdom guides me at every sleep I take .

Totally safe , I advance towards my highest good,

And I do it with joy and with ease.

I am a new person and i live in the world that I have chosen.

I deeply appreciate everything I have and all that I am .

Blessings and Prosperity come to me from everywhere.

Everything is fine in my world .. 🙏

Thank you !

Thank you !

Thank you !

AGGRESSIVE CHILDREN

If your child is very aggressive you can bless them with prayer..

The best time for blessings is when they are in deep sleep.

When someone is in deep sleep their conscious mind is not active and they accept the energies easily.

So keep your hands in the blessings position.

Stand in front of your child or you can assume (visualize) them in front of you.

And say...

"To the Supreme God,

I thank you for blessing my child (name) with your Divine light, guidance, love, mercy, healing, and good health, with inner strength, your divine help, and protection.

I thank you for blessing (name of the child) with Spirituality, Abundance, and Prosperity at all levels.

Om Shanti Shanti Om

Om Shanti Shanti Om

Om Shanti Shanti Om

Thank you in full faith.

God's blessings be to all"

GUPT NAVRATRI

Gupt Navratri, also known as Secret Navratri or Ashadha Navratri, is typically celebrated during the Hindu month of Ashadha, which falls in June or July of the Gregorian calendar. This lesser-known Navratri is observed with devotion and fasting by some devotees, but it is not as widely celebrated or recognized as the Chaitra and Sharad Navratri, which occur in the months of Chaitra (usually in March or April) and Ashwin (usually in September or October) respectively.

The exact dates for Gupt Navratri may vary each year based on the lunar calendar, so it's advisable to consult a Hindu calendar or a reliable source to determine the specific dates for Gupt Navratri in a particular year. During Gupt Navratri, devotees worship the goddess Durga and seek her blessings through various rituals and prayers, similar to the more well-known Navratri celebrations

During Gupt Navratri, devotees typically perform special pujas and rituals dedicated to the goddess Durga.

The reason for performing rituals during Gupt Navratri is to seek the blessings of the goddess Durga, who is believed to be particularly receptive during this time. It is considered an auspicious period for spiritual growth, purification, and seeking protection from negative energies. Devotees believe that by observing these rituals with sincerity and devotion, they can gain the goddess's favour and blessings, including protection from adversities and the removal of obstacles in their lives.

Special tantra are believed to be performed during gupt navratri.

NAVRATRI DAYS WISE:

DAY 1: MAA SHAILPUTRI

An incarnation of PARWATI. She is depicted as riding the bull (Nandi) with Trishula in her right hand and lotus in her left hand. Shailputri is considered to be the direct incarnation of Mahakali. She is worshiped for good health and releasing fear.

Chakra : basic\ root\ muladhar.

DAY 2: MAA BRAHMACHARINI

Maa signifies wisdom and knowledge. She holds rosary in her right hand and a kamandal in her left hand. She wears rudraksh. Goddess Brahmcharani blesses you with great emotional strength to keep your mental balance and confidence even in darkest hours.

Chakra : navel\ sacral

DAY 3: MAA CHANDRAGHANTA

The third manifestation of Devi Durga, she has a chandra or half moon, in a shape of bell on her forehead,

A symbol of peace, serenity and prosperity, Maa has three eyes and ten hands holding ten types of swords, weapons and arrows, she establishes justice and courage and strength to fight challenges and keep the negative energy away and repel all the trouble from your life.

Chakra : solar plexus\ manipur

DAY 4: MAA KUSHMANDA

She is considered the creator of the Universe. She has eight hands, with a jar of nectar(amrit) in one hand. Maa resides in the core of the sun and thus controls the Surya lok.

Maa Kushmanda helps to improve your health and wealth. She removes all the hurdles and troubles from our life. Improve our relationship.

Chakra : heart chakra

DAY 5: MAA SKANDAMATA

She is holding lord Skanda in his infant form and a lotus in her right hand. She is also worshiped in the form of Parwati, Maheshwari or Maa Gauri. Devi is the symbol of mother and son relationship. By worshipping her, you get immense love and affection from her and get all the desires fulfilled.

Chakra : throat chakra

DAY 6: MAA KATYAYNI

Maa Katyayni has three eyes and four hands. She holds a sword in her one left hand and a lotus in another. The other two hand respectively shows protection and allowing actions. Maa blesses you with better health and wealth, you develop great strength to fight all disease, sorrow and fear.

Chakra : ajna chakra\ third eye chakra.

DAY 7: MAA KALRATRI

Kaal means time and death and Kaalratri means the one who is death of kaal. Maa Kaalratri destroys ignorance and bring light into the dark. The super power that creates havoc and removes all things bad and dirty, she brings calmness and courage.

Chakra : forehead chakra.

DAY 8: MAA MAHAGAURI

She has three eyes and four hands, her lower right hand holds a Trishul and the upper right hand is in the mudra of allaying fear. Whereas her lower left hand is in a pose of granting boons to her devotees and she is holding a damaru in her upper left hand. She has a calming effect on lives of her devotees and also helps them to improve their knowledge.

Maa helps us leads to the path of virtue and inner power. Gives success and Ashwarya in life.

Chakra : crown chakra

DAY 9: MAA SHIDDHIDATRI

She is possessor of twenty six different wishes (siddhis) which she grants her worshipers. This avtar of Maa Durga removes ignorance and provides knowledge to her devotees. Maa sits on kamal(lotus) and rides on lion. Her glory and power are infinite and worshipping Maa Siddhidatri on the 9th day of Navratri bestows all siddhis to her devotees and also marks the successful completion of the Navratri festival.

WATER HEALING

Water has tremendous healing potential for the human mind, body and spirit. Water can physiologically and psychologically benefit people because of its therapeutic nature. For thousands of years it has been known to help cure illness, refresh the body and relax the mind.

Nothing is softer or more flexible than water, yet nothing can resist it —

Water is the most common substance on earth and is with us in every moment of our life. It is the most abundant compound on earth covering over 70% of the planet. The earth is a living dynamic being with veins and arteries and the water flowing through it is connected to one large thriving heart, or the ocean. Water evaporates and again comes back to earth in the form of rain, forms arteries and veins, and finally connects to the ocean. This constant circulation keeps the planet alive.

We are like the surface of earth and water makes up between 65% and 78% of our body (depending on age), comprising 70% of our brain, heart, skin, muscles, kidneys, lungs, and liver. Like our planet, it is water that gives us life. Adults consume about 2.5 litres of water each day. The more water we lose, the more we deteriorate and eventually, we die. We are thus water in the human form.

Water can change its form from solid to liquid into vapour and return to the liquid form. Besides this property, one of the most amazing qualities of water is that it holds memory and carries information. Its molecules are organised in clusters that work as 'memory cells,' so to speak. Within each memory cell, there are roughly 440,000 information panels that are responsible for the interaction with its environment, making it nature's single most malleable computer, according to late Rustom Roy, scientist and professor emeritus at the Pennsylvania State University.

Whatever water hears, sees, and feels becomes a catalyst for its change as it copies, memorises, and transports information.

Japanese researcher Masaru Emoto demonstrated this with his water crystal project. In this study, Emoto played music, displayed words, and prayed to water while it was freezing, and when the water was frozen it created crystal shapes distinct to each stimulus. When music were positive and loving, intricate crystal shapes appeared. On the contrary, when sounds and words were negative and harsh, chaotic, incoherent shapes formed.

This research is particularly interesting in the light of water's prevalence in our bodies. "Water serves as a transporter of energy throughout your body...carried by blood and bodily fluids, it is the means by which nourishment is circulated throughout our bodies...this flow of water enables us to live active lives,"

Studies have proven that water has live energy to it. Human beings are made of energy that is flowing through each and every cell of our body. Since water has the property of carrying memory and information, it being passed in our body becomes critical.

Water is alive when it is fresh from the springs, but the one that comes to us in the cities from the municipal pipes has already gone through a series of chemical processing and harsh treatment. The water that we flush enters into the sewage and is then recycled after chemical processing back to our homes into pipelines. The energy of water is depleted, and over a period of time and it becomes dead water.

Water also reacts to emotional exposure and the water we drink carries those emotions straight into the cells of our body. Humans may not come to know the difference between live spring water and chemically processed one, but pets and animals are more likely to choose natural, live water over the tap water as they are more in tune with natural energies.

When you consume water after the following methods, it will harmonise your body. It helps in healing migraines and provide therapeutic support to people suffering from diseases like cancer, diabetes, and certain kind of heart conditions.

1.Speak to water; before consuming water, hold the glass of water and send thoughts like, 'Thank you water, thank you for healing my body; I love you; thank you for nourishing my cells; I am happy and joyful.' Words have energy and carry a certain frequency and vibration. Love and gratitude vibrate at the highest frequency. Saying this for 2 to 5 minutes changes the frequency of water and when the water is consumed, it passes this information to the water molecules in the body. You can say this in your mind or even aloud.

2. Chant over water; it increases its vibration and frequency.

3. Play Mozart, Beethoven or other music; playing music at 428 Hz or 728 Hz frequencies can entrain molecules of water with resonance effect.

4. Pray over your food and water; it changes the frequency and energy of the food, thus making it more alive for the body.

They say that water is the best natural remedy and you can drink your way to better health.

🔛 "Charging water with the energy of abundance"

1. Pour distilled or boiled water into a glass.

2. Take the glass in your hand or, sitting comfortably, place the glass of water in front of you.

3. Close your eyes.

4. Start imagining pictures related to wealth, abundance and financial (imagine yourself a healthy person, for you it will be the elixir of health) prosperity.

Here your husband suddenly gives you a car, here you win a large sum of money in the lottery, but your boss writes you a bonus in the amount of two salaries.

Remember, your pictures should be positive, as well as closest to the realities of life.

However, you can also dream about the impossible.

After all, they say that dreaming is not harmful, but it is harmful - not to dream.

5. Now drink the water charged with the energy of abundance.

And drink it with full and unconditional

(imagine how water transforms all your illnesses into light) with the confidence that everything conceived for water will definitely come true!

6. Do not be surprised if life will make its own adjustments to your visualization plans. Rejoice in what you get thanks to the charmed water.

And next time, monetary luck will be more favourable to you.

7. You can perform this technique monthly.

WATER CODES

To balance the masculine and feminine energies, write these two numbers on opposite sides of the water container

99 77 654 and 44 66 111--this creates a vortex which puts healing into the water that one can drink to balance.

Negative energies can have an influence on our mental health, which makes it necessary for them to be eliminated with a spiritual routine. The ritual we have for you, involves placing a glass of water near the bed to eliminate bad vibes.

Water is one of the primary elements that can eliminate negative energies easily.

When you put a glass of water under your bed, the liquid will absorb all the negative energy in your room.

The next thing is to get rid of the water in the morning and change it for fresh water for the next night. You can repeat the process as many times as you want.

Way to perform this routine

As we already mentioned, the routine is very simple: just put water from the tap in a well-kept glass, then put the glass near the bed and leave it overnight.

Observe the glass in the morning: if it looks cloudy and the water has bubbles, it means that it has effectively absorbed the negative energy. Even if the glass is transparent and the water without a lot of bubbles, it must have absorbed the bad vibes.

The final step is to throw the water through the toilet and repeat the procedure, placing a glass of fresh water near the bed at night.

You should never use the same water from the previous night.

Keep the glass or container open.

Use glass only

No labels

Designs or anything intricated on it.

Flush once you wake up

Many say you can keep it under your bed also

Extended description

I imagine you'll be thinking ... How can something as simple as a glass of water solve our problems or change our lives? In response I can tell you: Who told us that life has to be always complicated and consequently why solving a problem has to always be the difficult way.

You have not thought that the simple and the complicated belong to a belief system and how we manage within this system, "Yes" it can become complicated to do something as simple as this Water Glass Ritual, since we are accustomed to always act looking for logic and choosing the most difficult paths.

Well, everything is a matter of deciding to do it, believe it or not, water has a great healing power and this belief is something that lasted in antiquity and today is proven by science.

So go ahead and do this Ritual of the Glass of Water and enjoy its therapeutic benefits:

1.- Take a glass cup, completely transparent and fill it 3/4 parts with tap water.

2.- Find a place in your home that makes you vibrate loudly. That makes you feel good and calm.

3.- You should do it in a moment of complete calm, where you are relaxed, alone and where no one can interrupt you.

4.- Leave your glass of water in that place you chose and start telling everything you feel. Talk about all your negative emotions: anger, sadness, frustration. Imagine that this is your best friend and you are telling him what happens to you.

When doing this, what is going to happen is that you are going to begin to take out of you situations that maybe you do not even imagine, that you had saved for a long time.

After doing this, you should repeat the following sentence: "Divinity ... clean in me the idea or belief that this problem has generated. I'm sorry, forgive me, thank you, I love you".

This you can do twice a day: once in the morning and once in the evening or once a day. But the intention is that you go pulling out everything that is inside you that is generating those negative feelings.

If you are going to practice it twice a day, you do it first thing in the morning. You leave the glass all day and in the night when you go back to carry out, you throw the water. You fill the glass again with water, you perform your ritual again and leave it overnight, and so on.

As you practice this ritual, you will begin to feel more and more relaxed and most likely, you will find the solution to the problem or situation that afflicts you.

Why does it work?

You are leaving in the glass, all that situation that is bothering you. You are doing a self-analysis. When you take everything out from within you, in some way you are cleaning what is in your conscious and in turn, help your subconscious to work and to get the real information that you need and that will make you feel at peace.

You will leave your problems in the glass, and the Divinity will be in charge of transmuting them, (this will be a way of letting go of those situations that you are living and that are disturbing you), to bring that perfect solution to all our problems, since those answers that we are looking, they are inside us. Remember, we are the creators of our reality and that is why the solutions to our problems will always be within us.

You may not believe in this. It is not worthwhile to discuss whether it is true or not. Everyone will have their opinion. I can only say that with experimenting you do not lose anything, but you can earn a lot. A peace beyond understanding.8Magnetizes Water: The Water of Life

In the morning, make a glass of clean water. Raise your left arm and place your palm face up, palm right over the glass, bless the water and say the following words:

"I am the Divine Presence that carries this water with the divine essence of life, which I drink now and that renews my bodies with perfect health and eternal youth."

Then drink the water, keeping the left hand upwards, and pass the right hand a few times over the belly, starting from the left side, going up to the arch of the ribs and then to the right side and down to the left groin.

This exercise should be performed exactly as described.

Try to keep in consciousness:

"I am the perfect activity of every organ and every cell of my body."

Say often:

"I am the perfect health that manifests itself in every organ of my body."Benefits of drinking water

Water keeps every system in the body functioning properly

Water has many important jobs, such as:

- carrying nutrients and oxygen to your cells
- flushing bacteria from your bladder
- aiding digestion
- preventing constipation
- normalizing blood pressure
- stabilizing the heartbeat

Prayer with sequences to charge the water: take a glass of water and holding it in your hands you begin to inform the water dear water I love you, normalize your structure.

51951348988 tell all the cells of my body to heal.

1814321 To rejuvenate.

2145432 Restoring my organs.

419312819212 collects in form.

91739421794159 and take away the tiredness giving rest to my body.

73918531791 totally regenerating my health.

5148517 I call the power of the creator in my life.

1231115025 With gratitude to the universe

5148123 thank you!

The water goes away, (can use this while taking a bath or can use your imagination)my troubles go away. As the water evaporates, my life changes. The Universe helps me today and improves my life. May it be so! Thank you !!!

LIVING WATER

Water is one of the most powerful elements. At the physical level, water dissolves many substances, at the energetic level it absorbs emotions, thoughts, programs.

Alchemists knew about the unique properties of water. Their knowledge has been confirmed by modern research. Water molecules are modified under the influence of different programs and emotions. If you say evil, offensive words, the molecules acquire certain outlines, respectively, the water molecules that have "heard" the words of love and tenderness also have their own pattern. The energy message that words contain is read and stored by water - like a memory device.

It turns out that we ourselves can charge water, endow it with virtually magical properties.

Energy therapists actively use this technique in their practice. So why don't we prepare for ourselves an almost magical elixir - water charged for a positive, for the fulfillment of desires?

Fill a glass with water. Bend over him and say the code phrase (for example: "my income is constantly growing", "I am happy", "my man finds me", "I am healthy", "my life is full of joy", etc.). Write the same phrase on two pieces of paper. Put a glass of water on one, cover the glass on top with the other. The information of the words spoken and written has the same wave frequency and energy, so the water counts the information twice. Gradually, the water will be recharged and, as a result, will accumulate a large charge of positive energy. After a day, the concentration of the charge will reach its maximum. Drink this water and wait for a change. Happy events will surely happen, do not hesitate!

WATER TREATMENT

Water is a unique substance. Its properties are simply amazing. Water on our planet is found in three states of aggregation, its physical properties contributed to the origin of life. However, the study of water continues, and its secrets have not yet been revealed. More has become known over the past 20 years. For example, water burns, and the most amazing thing is that it has a memory.

The structure of water is such that it can record any information. This information is stored in a special structure - clusters. Whether it's a good word or a sent swear word: she absorbs everything. You can erase such messages at the moment the liquid passes from one phase to another, that is, during melting, boiling, etc. etc. Having purified the water in this way, we can write down anything we want in its memory.

Fill the container with water, previously "informationally purified". In a calm atmosphere, mentally, or better aloud, say your wish. You need to speak in an even voice. Prayer is best. Wait a couple of minutes and drink a glass of water. Do this regularly. Even 10 grams of structured water added to 50 liters of plain water will turn it into healing water.

"A kind word is pleasant to the cat," the people say. This is not far from the truth. Say a good word to the water, drink it and feel yourself a surge of energy. A properly structured liquid will instantly react with your own and the result will not be long in coming. A person is 70-90% water. We begin life surrounded by amniotic fluid. The most painful death is from thirst.

Any thought can be formulated in water. Anyone who drinks such water will automatically be imbued with the meaning of your desire. You can heal any disease, turn any source into drinkable. There are plenty of facts to support these arguments. However, science still cannot fully use the discovery of the memory of water in any channel. One thing can be said with firmness - this is not mysticism. This is already science. Even fruits and vegetables, watered with the "right" water, ripen faster and give a larger yield, which the breeders have already taken note of.

With this knowledge, a person can accomplish a lot. Some scientists, for example, are inclined to believe that all cataclysms are the result of human emotions. All anger, anger, envy accumulate in the water, which cannot cope with such a flow of negativity and turns against its creators in the form of tsunamis, hurricanes, etc. Thus, the water is purified.

Have we thought about this while preparing food, swimming? .. Any word carries information. Only a liquid with a natural structure and strength is capable of working miracles in the body. She can heal you from any ailment, help you lose or gain weight, find peace of mind. To achieve the desired result with water, you must follow a number of simple tricks. Never speak or think badly while eating or preparing food. Always wish people well. While drinking a glass of water, or offering it to others, read a prayer over it or say a kind word.

Leave drinking water in a room where classical music is playing. After a month of drinking only such water, you will feel like just a different person. If you have to drink from an unknown source, say 2 words: love and gratitude. This is the most powerful spell that purifies the energy of water.

Your well-being will noticeably improve. Be healthy and may love and gratitude accompany you.

MONEY SHOWER RITUAL

You only need a bathroom with a shower. And, of course, high spirits and faith in Miracles!

Turn on the shower, make a strong pressure and stand so that the jets of water hit the top of your head. Close your eyes for a minute and imagine how falling drops turn into ringing coins and you are under the flow of universal abundance! For a full minute you are connected to an inexhaustible source of money energy! You are standing in the pouring rain of money! Wait for the peak of the emotionality of your feelings and say out loud three times: "I am the center of attraction for money!"

Take a magic shower at least twice a day - in the morning and in the evening - and be sure that your financial situation will change quickly and money will find you!

How to enhance the effect of the "money shower"?

To speed up the process and increase efficiency, once a week or a month, it is recommended to enhance the effect of the ritual.

Charging with water energy

Water is a living substance, scientists of the world have already proven how it reacts to external vibrations, changing its structure. Mandala, as a conductor of high-frequency vibrations, can have a positive effect on water, structuring it in a special way, creating from "dead water" (that is, having lost its structure and therefore not very useful for health) into "living". Pour raw water into a glass vessel in the evening, cover it with the image of your choice (you can also attach the image to the bottom or side of the container with water) and mentally or aloud formulate your desire-intention, which may be: "Let this water recharge with energy, which will cleanse it of all harmful impurities, let it remove toxins from my body, help get rid of ... (list your diseases), calm the nervous system, bring the highest benefit for me. "

It is necessary that all wishes-intentions that you formulate are extremely sincere and uttered with faith in success. Usually the water is ready for use within a few hours. To enhance the effect, you can use several images, at once, for example, one covering the vessel on top, and placing the other at the bottom, etc.

Water charged in this way is suitable for cooking, dough, compotes, watering flowers, etc. If you bathe your baby in such water, your baby will be calmer, his skin will be cleansed and he will develop better. It is recommended to drink this water for both children and adults.

You can use charged water as a "concentrate" by adding a small amount of it to ordinary water, so all the water after a while will absorb the charged energy and become structured.

Here's the technique:

"I can offer one powerful technique. Write a thought form on a piece of paper. For example: "I am a very charming person. An inner light of charm, love and light emanates from me. I am a luminous being. My man finds me. " Place a glass of water on this piece of paper. Rub your palms, move them like an accordion, imagine between your palms a full energy like a balloon. This is your energy. Place the glass between your palms without touching it. Speak consciously and with conviction this thought form, imagining its meaning if possible. Then drink some water. Do this in the morning after waking up and in the evening before bed. Your intention will be realized.

We write information on the water

So, how can you cleanse the water of all negative information and write down positive information on it so that the water acquires healing properties?

Thought forms for cleansing and charging water:

1. Place a glass of water on the palm of your left hand, and with your right hand cover the glass from above.

2. With the power of your mind, begin to transfer energy from your hands to water, say to yourself or aloud the following words, thought forms:

3. I start a program to neutralize all harmful chemical impurities, heavy metal salts in this water.

4. The composition of salts and microelements necessary for the normalization of my health remains in the water.

5. All pathogens, bacteria, protozoa and other parasites are neutralized with this water.

6. This water is programmed to cleanse the body of toxins, pathogenic bacteria and other parasites.

7. Give the water positive emotions of love and gratitude, set a positive intention, for example, "Water - give health, give strength, give energy, restore my health, restore every cell of my body!"

8. Turn on your imagination, write down on the water the information that will be most appropriate for you, for example:

I program this water to cleanse all the vessels in my body.

To restore vision.

Resorption of glaucoma, cataracts.

To restore the health of my heart.

To restore potency.

To eliminate sand in the kidneys, salts in the joints.

Resorption of tumors, fibroids, cysts.

To eliminate toothache or headache, etc.

EVERYTHING YOU RESOLUTELY SPEAK WITH FAITH, WATER WILL RECEIVE AND WRITE DOWN. "

You can just say to the water: "I love you. I thank you," just say not with your mind, but with your soul, your heart!

Drink this water and restore your health!

Finding yourself on the street in rain or snow, raise your hands with your palms up and say: "Rain (snow) from heaven - money in my pocket!" Regularly "feed" your wallet with electricity using a charger for mobile phones (put the plug in the compartment for notes).

How to get energized

Water

The easiest way to do this at home is while taking a shower or bath, to approach this process not mechanically, but consciously, saying an affirmation to yourself or aloud:

"Water, take away from my life, from my body and aura, all negative information, all unnecessary thoughts and attitudes, all illnesses and failures. Make me more harmonious, calm and balanced. Fill me with energy and strength. "

If you are in nature, where there is an open reservoir, then the effect of performing this technique will be even stronger. Whenever possible, swim in open bodies of water as often as possible, doing it consciously and being filled with the power of the elements.

How to prepare money water to attract wealth to your home?

There is a proven method by which you can forget about the problems associated with money. Cash water for cleaning floors. You need to put coins in a bowl or bucket for cleaning floors. Pre-wash them with water and salt to renew their energy. Then fill the money with clean water and let it "brew" for at least half an hour. Add a few drops of lemon, patchouli oil, or sandalwood if desired. On the bucket itself, you can write the words "raspberries" so that life is raspberries, "chocolate" so that "chocolate" is "honey" so that life is just as sweet. It is best to start cleaning floors in the farthest room and finish in front of the front door. At the same time, think that you will run out of money problems, and lure money out loud: "I wash the floor with water, I attract money into the house. I wash, cleanse, free the way for riches ". Water can be thrown out, and the money can be rinsed and put into a wallet so that the monetary energy is always with you. This water can be used to clean not only floors, but also all surfaces: doors, windows, walls. And one more way is easier, When you wash the floor, say to yourself: "I wash the floors of the house, I attract wealth to myself"

TECHNIQUE "GLASS OF WATER"

is considered a fairly effective way to achieve what you want, and this is explained not only by mysticism, but also by science. Water is a source of strength, a substance from which life in the Universe originated, therefore special, even magical properties are attributed to it.

1. Water receives and transmits information. The past, present and future are dissolved in water. She can record and save any information. This is due to clusters that change their shape under the influence of the surrounding world. This property of water has been widely used in the past and is used in the present: people continue to whisper and speak to water;

2. Water absorbs and retains energy. It is known that water is capable of absorbing cosmic energy and transmitting it in its pure form. It also absorbs human energy and lends itself to any "programming". And if you drink the "programmed" water, then it will give a signal for action.

Technique "Glass of water"

It is possible to speed up the fulfillment of desires in any area, be it relationships, health, beauty, business, self-realization or creativity. The most important thing is to decide and come up with any thought-form that conveys your intention.

• Get a glass of water. Water should be "live", not boiled, not bottled, but "live", from a fontanelle or well;

• Write your wish on the sheet. Desire should be written in the present tense, without the "not" particle, in an affirmative form and extremely concrete. It is recommended to imagine in paints that the dream has come true: to feel emotions, feel them and bring them through yourself;

• Collect energy. Rub your palms together, imagining that you are gathering energy around you. Feel warmth and a slight tingling sensation in the palms;

• Charge the water. Place the glass on top of the sheet with the written wish. Place your palms on the sides of the glass without touching it. Wait a minute or two, let your energy go into the water and charge it;

• Voice your desire. Speak your intention with confidence and awareness, feeling every word, passing every letter through yourself;

• Drink charged water. Drink slowly and with pleasure, wholly and completely surrendering to the moment. And then return to your usual life, with its affairs, as well as with new achievements and successes.

To improve your health, take a sheet of paper of any size and write "My health".

Hang your artwork on the wall and come up to it regularly and correct it. "I improve my health, I heal my body"

We get under the shower, imagining that we wash off our ailment and say: "The water washes my illness, cleans away the negativity."

SELF-TUNING

From that moment on, healing starts in me.

I feel a surge of strength with every breath.

My body is transforming through Love and acceptance.

I thank, let go of all the diseases that were in me and awakened me.

I feel how the joy of life revitalizes and rejuvenates me.

All the cells of my body begin to work for the transformation and transformation of the body.

I can feel the energy of life filling my vessel.

I accept with gratitude everything that the Creator gives me.

I am healthy, happy and enjoying life

From that moment I learned that Life is beautiful.

I begin to live in harmony and balance.

Thank you and carry on the Light of Love and Transformation.

Thankyou

Place a glass of water in front of you and mentally say the affirmation: "I AM A MONEY MAGNET" or "MONEY COMES FREQUENTLY AND EASY".

You can come up with something of your own. The main thing is to be brief and to the point.

Keep your hands around the glass and mentally charge the water to

the way that spoken affirmation evokes in you. When

feel (just feel) that the water is already charged, drink it and

feel how every cell of your body is saturated with energy

money, as every cell becomes a magnet for money. Imagine

how money sticks to you, how it revolves around you.

PRACTICE "MAGIC ELIXIR"

Here's a good and very simple practice for you!

She will help to always be in a good mood,

confident and healthy!

Practice "Magic Elixir".

Make yourself some tea, fresh juice, or maybe just pour water into a cup.

You can use one hand, or you can hug the cup with two and say something positive about the water.

For example: "I am always accompanied by luck, success and wealth",

"I love and be loved", "in my life there is always everything that I want",

or whatever you want. Then drink the charged liquid.

It has long been known that water absorbs information very well.

When such water enters your body, the information of love, success, wealth, abundance permeates every cell of your body.

You can do this not only for yourself, but also for your loved ones.

Say it every time you drink water:

"Pure water, holy water, water created by God enters my cells and they are healed"

Norma

394 868 466 87

1489999

www.ingramcontent.com/pod-product-compliance
Lightning Source LLC
LaVergne TN
LVHW061555070526
838199LV00077B/7057